# Global Salads: 50 Recipes for Every Occasion

By: Kelly Johnson

# Table of Contents

- Greek Salad
- Caesar Salad
- Caprese Salad
- Thai Papaya Salad
- Mexican Street Corn Salad
- Moroccan Carrot Salad
- Japanese Seaweed Salad
- Israeli Salad
- Indian Kachumber Salad
- Korean Kimchi Salad
- French Nicoise Salad
- Italian Panzanella
- German Potato Salad
- Lebanese Fattoush
- Vietnamese Goi Cuon Salad
- Brazilian Mango and Avocado Salad
- Egyptian Fattah Salad
- Chinese Cucumber Salad
- Spanish Ensalada Mixta
- Turkish Shepherd's Salad
- Jamaican Jerk Chicken Salad
- Mediterranean Quinoa Salad
- Russian Olivier Salad
- Peruvian Avocado Salad
- Scandinavian Beet and Apple Salad
- Cuban Black Bean Salad
- Filipino Ensaladang Mangga
- Thai Beef Salad
- Nigerian Jollof Rice Salad
- Sri Lankan Coconut Salad
- Lebanese Tabbouleh
- South African Potato Salad
- Swedish Creamy Cabbage Salad
- Indonesian Gado-Gado Salad
- Hawaiian Ahi Poke Salad

- Malaysian Rojak Salad
- Belgian Endive Salad
- Finnish Root Vegetable Salad
- Australian Beetroot and Goat Cheese Salad
- Argentine Grilled Corn Salad
- Chilean Avocado and Tomato Salad
- Dutch Apple Salad
- Middle Eastern Lentil Salad
- New Zealand Kumara Salad
- Canadian Caesar Salad
- Egyptian Tabbouleh
- Colombian Mango Salad
- Turkish Lentil Salad
- Indian Chana Salad
- Mexican Cucumber and Lime Salad

## Greek Salad

**Ingredients:**

- 1 cucumber, diced
- 2 tomatoes, chopped
- 1 red onion, thinly sliced
- 1 bell pepper, chopped
- 1/2 cup Kalamata olives
- 1/2 cup feta cheese, cubed
- 2 tablespoons olive oil
- 1 tablespoon red wine vinegar
- 1 teaspoon dried oregano
- Salt and pepper, to taste

**Instructions:**

1. In a large bowl, combine the cucumber, tomatoes, onion, bell pepper, olives, and feta cheese.
2. In a small bowl, whisk together the olive oil, red wine vinegar, oregano, salt, and pepper.
3. Drizzle the dressing over the salad and toss to combine.
4. Serve immediately or chill for 30 minutes before serving for enhanced flavor.

**Caesar Salad**

**Ingredients:**

- 4 cups Romaine lettuce, chopped
- 1/2 cup Caesar dressing
- 1/4 cup Parmesan cheese, grated
- Croutons, to taste
- Freshly ground black pepper, to taste

**Instructions:**

1. In a large bowl, toss the Romaine lettuce with Caesar dressing.
2. Add Parmesan cheese and croutons, and toss gently.
3. Season with freshly ground black pepper and serve immediately.

## Caprese Salad

**Ingredients:**

- 4 ripe tomatoes, sliced
- 1 ball of fresh mozzarella, sliced
- 1/4 cup fresh basil leaves
- 2 tablespoons extra virgin olive oil
- 1 tablespoon balsamic glaze
- Salt and pepper, to taste

**Instructions:**

1. Arrange the tomato and mozzarella slices alternately on a plate.
2. Tuck basil leaves between the tomato and mozzarella slices.
3. Drizzle with olive oil and balsamic glaze.
4. Sprinkle with salt and pepper, and serve immediately.

## Thai Papaya Salad (Som Tum)

**Ingredients:**

- 2 cups shredded green papaya
- 1/2 cup cherry tomatoes, halved
- 1/4 cup green beans, cut into 2-inch pieces
- 2-3 Thai bird's eye chilies (adjust to taste)
- 2 cloves garlic, minced
- 1 tablespoon palm sugar
- 2 tablespoons fish sauce
- 1 tablespoon lime juice
- 1 tablespoon roasted peanuts, crushed
- Fresh cilantro, for garnish

**Instructions:**

1. In a mortar and pestle, pound the chilies, garlic, and palm sugar together until fragrant.
2. Add the fish sauce, lime juice, and a little water to make the dressing.
3. In a large bowl, combine the shredded papaya, tomatoes, and green beans.
4. Pour the dressing over the papaya mixture and toss to combine.
5. Garnish with crushed peanuts and cilantro. Serve immediately.

## Mexican Street Corn Salad (Esquites)

**Ingredients:**

- 4 cups corn kernels (fresh or frozen)
- 1 tablespoon butter
- 1/4 cup mayonnaise
- 1 tablespoon sour cream
- 1 tablespoon lime juice
- 1 teaspoon chili powder
- 1/4 cup Cotija cheese, crumbled
- 2 tablespoons fresh cilantro, chopped
- Salt and pepper, to taste

**Instructions:**

1. Heat a large skillet over medium heat and melt the butter.
2. Add the corn kernels and cook, stirring occasionally, until slightly charred, about 5-7 minutes.
3. Remove the corn from the heat and let it cool slightly.
4. In a large bowl, combine the mayonnaise, sour cream, lime juice, chili powder, and season with salt and pepper.
5. Add the corn to the bowl and toss to coat evenly.
6. Garnish with Cotija cheese and cilantro before serving.

## Moroccan Carrot Salad

**Ingredients:**

- 4 large carrots, peeled and grated
- 1/4 cup fresh parsley, chopped
- 1 tablespoon olive oil
- 1 tablespoon lemon juice
- 1 teaspoon ground cumin
- 1 teaspoon honey
- Salt and pepper, to taste

**Instructions:**

1. In a large bowl, combine the grated carrots and parsley.
2. In a small bowl, whisk together the olive oil, lemon juice, cumin, honey, salt, and pepper.
3. Drizzle the dressing over the carrot mixture and toss well.
4. Serve chilled or at room temperature.

## Japanese Seaweed Salad

**Ingredients:**

- 2 cups mixed seaweed (wakame, hijiki, or kombu)
- 2 tablespoons rice vinegar
- 1 tablespoon soy sauce
- 1 teaspoon sesame oil
- 1/2 teaspoon sugar
- 1 teaspoon sesame seeds
- 1 green onion, thinly sliced
- 1 tablespoon shredded carrots (optional)

**Instructions:**

1. Soak the seaweed in warm water for 5-10 minutes, then drain and rinse.
2. In a small bowl, whisk together the rice vinegar, soy sauce, sesame oil, and sugar.
3. Toss the seaweed with the dressing and sprinkle with sesame seeds, green onion, and shredded carrots (if using).
4. Serve immediately or refrigerate for 30 minutes to enhance the flavor.

## Israeli Salad

**Ingredients:**

- 2 cucumbers, diced
- 2 tomatoes, diced
- 1/4 red onion, finely chopped
- 1/4 cup fresh parsley, chopped
- 2 tablespoons olive oil
- 1 tablespoon lemon juice
- Salt and pepper, to taste

**Instructions:**

1. In a large bowl, combine the cucumbers, tomatoes, onion, and parsley.
2. Drizzle with olive oil and lemon juice.
3. Season with salt and pepper and toss gently.
4. Serve immediately or refrigerate for 30 minutes to enhance the flavor.

## Indian Kachumber Salad

**Ingredients:**

- 1 cucumber, diced
- 1 tomato, diced
- 1/4 red onion, finely chopped
- 1/2 green chili, finely chopped (optional)
- 1 tablespoon fresh cilantro, chopped
- 1 tablespoon lemon juice
- 1/2 teaspoon cumin powder
- Salt and pepper, to taste

**Instructions:**

1. In a large bowl, combine the cucumber, tomato, onion, and green chili (if using).
2. Add the cilantro, lemon juice, cumin powder, salt, and pepper.
3. Toss well and serve immediately.

## Korean Kimchi Salad

**Ingredients:**

- 1 cup kimchi, chopped
- 2 cups napa cabbage, shredded
- 1/2 cucumber, julienned
- 1 carrot, julienned
- 2 tablespoons sesame oil
- 1 tablespoon rice vinegar
- 1 teaspoon soy sauce
- 1 teaspoon sugar
- 1 tablespoon sesame seeds
- 2 green onions, chopped
- 1/2 teaspoon red pepper flakes (optional)

**Instructions:**

1. In a large bowl, combine the chopped kimchi, napa cabbage, cucumber, and carrot.
2. In a small bowl, whisk together the sesame oil, rice vinegar, soy sauce, and sugar.
3. Pour the dressing over the salad and toss to combine.
4. Sprinkle sesame seeds, green onions, and red pepper flakes (if using) on top.
5. Serve immediately or chill for 30 minutes for enhanced flavor.

**French Nicoise Salad**

**Ingredients:**

- 2 cups mixed salad greens
- 1/2 cup cherry tomatoes, halved
- 1/4 red onion, thinly sliced
- 2 hard-boiled eggs, quartered
- 1/2 cup cooked green beans
- 1/2 cup Kalamata olives
- 1/4 cup tuna (canned or fresh)
- 2 tablespoons olive oil
- 1 tablespoon red wine vinegar
- 1 teaspoon Dijon mustard
- Salt and pepper, to taste

**Instructions:**

1. Arrange the salad greens, tomatoes, red onion, eggs, green beans, olives, and tuna on a platter.
2. In a small bowl, whisk together olive oil, red wine vinegar, Dijon mustard, salt, and pepper.
3. Drizzle the dressing over the salad and serve immediately.

**Italian Panzanella**

**Ingredients:**

- 4 cups cubed stale bread (preferably sourdough or baguette)
- 2 ripe tomatoes, diced
- 1 cucumber, diced
- 1/4 red onion, thinly sliced
- 1/4 cup fresh basil leaves, chopped
- 3 tablespoons olive oil
- 2 tablespoons red wine vinegar
- 1 teaspoon sugar
- Salt and pepper, to taste

**Instructions:**

1. In a large bowl, combine the bread cubes, tomatoes, cucumber, red onion, and basil.
2. In a small bowl, whisk together olive oil, red wine vinegar, sugar, salt, and pepper.
3. Pour the dressing over the bread mixture and toss to combine.
4. Let the salad sit for about 15 minutes for the flavors to meld, then serve.

## German Potato Salad

**Ingredients:**

- 6 medium potatoes, boiled and sliced
- 1/2 cup cooked bacon, crumbled
- 1/4 cup chopped green onions
- 1/4 cup fresh parsley, chopped
- 1/2 cup apple cider vinegar
- 1/4 cup olive oil
- 1 tablespoon Dijon mustard
- 1/2 teaspoon sugar
- Salt and pepper, to taste

**Instructions:**

1. In a large bowl, combine the sliced potatoes, crumbled bacon, green onions, and parsley.
2. In a small bowl, whisk together the vinegar, olive oil, Dijon mustard, sugar, salt, and pepper.
3. Pour the dressing over the potato mixture and toss gently.
4. Serve immediately or chill for 30 minutes to enhance the flavor.

## Lebanese Fattoush

**Ingredients:**

- 4 cups mixed salad greens
- 1 cucumber, diced
- 1 tomato, diced
- 1/4 red onion, thinly sliced
- 1/4 cup fresh parsley, chopped
- 1/4 cup fresh mint, chopped
- 2 tablespoons pomegranate seeds (optional)
- 1/4 cup olive oil
- 2 tablespoons lemon juice
- 1 tablespoon pomegranate molasses (optional)
- 2 tablespoons sumac
- Salt and pepper, to taste
- 1-2 pieces of pita bread, toasted and crumbled

**Instructions:**

1. In a large bowl, combine the salad greens, cucumber, tomato, onion, parsley, mint, and pomegranate seeds (if using).
2. In a small bowl, whisk together olive oil, lemon juice, pomegranate molasses (if using), sumac, salt, and pepper.
3. Drizzle the dressing over the salad and toss to combine.
4. Top with the crumbled toasted pita bread and serve immediately.

**Vietnamese Goi Cuon Salad (Spring Roll Salad)**

**Ingredients:**

- 1 cup shredded lettuce
- 1 cup shredded cabbage
- 1/2 cup cooked shrimp, sliced
- 1/2 cucumber, julienned
- 1/4 cup fresh mint leaves, chopped
- 1/4 cup fresh cilantro leaves, chopped
- 1/4 cup roasted peanuts, crushed
- 2 tablespoons hoisin sauce
- 1 tablespoon rice vinegar
- 1 tablespoon soy sauce
- 1 teaspoon sugar
- 1 teaspoon lime juice

**Instructions:**

1. In a large bowl, combine the lettuce, cabbage, shrimp, cucumber, mint, and cilantro.
2. In a small bowl, whisk together hoisin sauce, rice vinegar, soy sauce, sugar, and lime juice.
3. Drizzle the dressing over the salad and toss to combine.
4. Top with crushed peanuts and serve immediately.

**Brazilian Mango and Avocado Salad**

**Ingredients:**

- 1 ripe mango, diced
- 1 avocado, diced
- 1/4 red onion, thinly sliced
- 1/4 cup fresh cilantro, chopped
- 1 tablespoon olive oil
- 1 tablespoon lime juice
- Salt and pepper, to taste

**Instructions:**

1. In a large bowl, combine the mango, avocado, red onion, and cilantro.
2. Drizzle with olive oil and lime juice, and season with salt and pepper.
3. Gently toss to combine and serve immediately.

**Egyptian Fattah Salad**

**Ingredients:**

- 2 cups mixed salad greens
- 1 cucumber, diced
- 2 tomatoes, diced
- 1/4 cup red onion, finely chopped
- 2 tablespoons fresh parsley, chopped
- 2 tablespoons tahini
- 2 tablespoons lemon juice
- 1 tablespoon olive oil
- Salt and pepper, to taste

**Instructions:**

1. In a large bowl, combine the salad greens, cucumber, tomatoes, red onion, and parsley.
2. In a small bowl, whisk together tahini, lemon juice, olive oil, salt, and pepper.
3. Drizzle the dressing over the salad and toss gently.
4. Serve immediately or chill for a more flavorful result.

**Chinese Cucumber Salad**

**Ingredients:**

- 2 cucumbers, thinly sliced
- 2 cloves garlic, minced
- 1 tablespoon sesame oil
- 2 tablespoons rice vinegar
- 1 tablespoon soy sauce
- 1 teaspoon sugar
- 1/2 teaspoon chili flakes (optional)
- 1 tablespoon sesame seeds
- 2 green onions, chopped

**Instructions:**

1. Place the sliced cucumbers in a bowl. Sprinkle with a pinch of salt and let them sit for 10 minutes to release excess water. Then, pat dry with a paper towel.
2. In a small bowl, whisk together sesame oil, rice vinegar, soy sauce, sugar, and chili flakes (if using).
3. Pour the dressing over the cucumbers and toss to coat evenly.
4. Sprinkle with sesame seeds and green onions. Serve chilled.

## Spanish Ensalada Mixta

**Ingredients:**

- 2 cups mixed salad greens
- 1/2 red onion, thinly sliced
- 2 tomatoes, chopped
- 1 cucumber, sliced
- 1/4 cup olives (green or black)
- 1/4 cup canned tuna, drained (optional)
- 2 tablespoons olive oil
- 1 tablespoon red wine vinegar
- Salt and pepper, to taste

**Instructions:**

1. In a large bowl, combine the salad greens, red onion, tomatoes, cucumber, olives, and tuna (if using).
2. In a small bowl, whisk together olive oil, red wine vinegar, salt, and pepper.
3. Drizzle the dressing over the salad and toss gently. Serve immediately.

**Turkish Shepherd's Salad (Çoban Salatası)**

**Ingredients:**

- 2 cucumbers, diced
- 2 tomatoes, diced
- 1/4 red onion, thinly sliced
- 1/4 cup fresh parsley, chopped
- 1/4 cup olive oil
- 2 tablespoons lemon juice
- Salt and pepper, to taste
- 1/4 teaspoon dried oregano (optional)

**Instructions:**

1. In a large bowl, combine the cucumbers, tomatoes, red onion, and parsley.
2. In a small bowl, whisk together olive oil, lemon juice, salt, pepper, and oregano (if using).
3. Pour the dressing over the salad and toss to combine. Serve immediately.

## Jamaican Jerk Chicken Salad

**Ingredients:**

- 2 cups mixed salad greens
- 1 chicken breast, grilled and sliced
- 1/2 red bell pepper, diced
- 1/2 cucumber, sliced
- 1/4 cup red onion, thinly sliced
- 1/4 cup mango, diced
- 1/4 cup jerk dressing or marinade
- 2 tablespoons olive oil
- Salt and pepper, to taste

**Instructions:**

1. Grill the chicken breast and slice it into strips.
2. In a large bowl, combine the mixed greens, red bell pepper, cucumber, red onion, and mango.
3. Add the grilled chicken on top.
4. Drizzle with jerk dressing or marinade, olive oil, and season with salt and pepper.
5. Toss to combine and serve immediately.

## Mediterranean Quinoa Salad

**Ingredients:**

- 1 cup cooked quinoa
- 1 cup cherry tomatoes, halved
- 1/2 cucumber, diced
- 1/4 red onion, finely chopped
- 1/4 cup Kalamata olives, sliced
- 1/4 cup feta cheese, crumbled
- 2 tablespoons olive oil
- 1 tablespoon lemon juice
- 1 teaspoon dried oregano
- Salt and pepper, to taste

**Instructions:**

1. In a large bowl, combine the quinoa, tomatoes, cucumber, red onion, olives, and feta cheese.
2. In a small bowl, whisk together olive oil, lemon juice, oregano, salt, and pepper.
3. Pour the dressing over the salad and toss gently. Serve chilled or at room temperature.

## Russian Olivier Salad

**Ingredients:**

- 2 potatoes, boiled and diced
- 2 carrots, boiled and diced
- 1/2 cup peas (frozen or canned)
- 3 hard-boiled eggs, diced
- 1/2 cup pickles, diced
- 1/2 cup mayonnaise
- Salt and pepper, to taste

**Instructions:**

1. In a large bowl, combine the boiled potatoes, carrots, peas, eggs, and pickles.
2. Add mayonnaise and stir gently to combine.
3. Season with salt and pepper to taste.
4. Chill in the fridge for at least 30 minutes before serving.

**Peruvian Avocado Salad**

**Ingredients:**

- 2 avocados, diced
- 1 tomato, diced
- 1/2 red onion, thinly sliced
- 1/4 cup fresh cilantro, chopped
- 1 tablespoon lime juice
- 1 tablespoon olive oil
- Salt and pepper, to taste

**Instructions:**

1. In a bowl, combine the diced avocados, tomato, red onion, and cilantro.
2. Drizzle with lime juice and olive oil. Season with salt and pepper.
3. Toss gently to combine and serve immediately.

## Scandinavian Beet and Apple Salad

**Ingredients:**

- 2 beets, boiled and diced
- 1 apple, diced
- 1/4 red onion, thinly sliced
- 1 tablespoon apple cider vinegar
- 2 tablespoons olive oil
- Salt and pepper, to taste
- Fresh dill, for garnish (optional)

**Instructions:**

1. In a large bowl, combine the boiled beets, apple, and red onion.
2. In a small bowl, whisk together apple cider vinegar, olive oil, salt, and pepper.
3. Drizzle the dressing over the salad and toss to combine.
4. Garnish with fresh dill, if desired, and serve immediately.

## Cuban Black Bean Salad

**Ingredients:**

- 2 cups cooked black beans (or 1 can, drained and rinsed)
- 1/2 red onion, finely chopped
- 1/2 red bell pepper, chopped
- 1/4 cup fresh cilantro, chopped
- 1 lime, juiced
- 2 tablespoons olive oil
- 1 teaspoon ground cumin
- Salt and pepper, to taste
- 1 avocado, diced (optional)

**Instructions:**

1. In a large bowl, combine the black beans, red onion, red bell pepper, and cilantro.
2. In a small bowl, whisk together lime juice, olive oil, cumin, salt, and pepper.
3. Pour the dressing over the salad and toss gently to combine.
4. Add avocado just before serving, if desired.

## Filipino Ensaladang Mangga

**Ingredients:**

- 2 ripe mangoes, peeled and sliced thinly
- 1 red onion, thinly sliced
- 1 cucumber, thinly sliced
- 1/4 cup fish sauce or soy sauce
- 1 tablespoon sugar
- 1 tablespoon vinegar
- 1/4 teaspoon chili flakes (optional)
- 1 tablespoon fresh cilantro, chopped

**Instructions:**

1. In a bowl, combine the mangoes, red onion, and cucumber.
2. In a small bowl, mix together the fish sauce or soy sauce, sugar, vinegar, and chili flakes (if using).
3. Pour the dressing over the salad and toss gently.
4. Garnish with fresh cilantro before serving.

## Thai Beef Salad

**Ingredients:**

- 1 lb beef steak (such as sirloin or flank), grilled and sliced thinly
- 1 cucumber, sliced thinly
- 1 carrot, julienned
- 1 red onion, thinly sliced
- 1/2 cup fresh cilantro, chopped
- 1/4 cup fresh mint, chopped
- 2 tablespoons lime juice
- 2 tablespoons fish sauce
- 1 tablespoon sugar
- 1-2 fresh chilies, sliced (optional)
- 1 tablespoon roasted peanuts, chopped (optional)

**Instructions:**

1. Grill the beef steak to your desired level of doneness, then slice thinly against the grain.
2. In a large bowl, combine the sliced beef, cucumber, carrot, red onion, cilantro, and mint.
3. In a small bowl, whisk together lime juice, fish sauce, sugar, and chilies.
4. Pour the dressing over the salad and toss to combine.
5. Garnish with chopped peanuts before serving.

## Nigerian Jollof Rice Salad

**Ingredients:**

- 2 cups cooked rice (preferably long-grain)
- 1/2 cup red bell pepper, diced
- 1/2 cup cucumber, diced
- 1/2 cup tomatoes, diced
- 1/4 cup red onion, finely chopped
- 1/4 cup olive oil
- 1 tablespoon vinegar
- 1 teaspoon ground thyme
- 1 teaspoon curry powder
- Salt and pepper, to taste
- Fresh parsley or cilantro, for garnish

**Instructions:**

1. In a large bowl, combine the cooked rice, red bell pepper, cucumber, tomatoes, and red onion.
2. In a small bowl, whisk together olive oil, vinegar, thyme, curry powder, salt, and pepper.
3. Pour the dressing over the rice and toss gently.
4. Garnish with fresh parsley or cilantro before serving.

**Sri Lankan Coconut Salad**

**Ingredients:**

- 1 cup fresh coconut, grated
- 1/2 cucumber, sliced
- 1/2 carrot, julienned
- 1 small red onion, sliced thinly
- 1-2 green chilies, sliced (optional)
- 2 tablespoons fresh lime juice
- Salt to taste
- Fresh cilantro or mint for garnish

**Instructions:**

1. In a large bowl, combine grated coconut, cucumber, carrot, onion, and green chilies (if using).
2. Add lime juice and salt to taste.
3. Toss to combine and garnish with fresh cilantro or mint before serving.

## Lebanese Tabbouleh

**Ingredients:**

- 1/2 cup bulgur wheat
- 2 tomatoes, diced
- 1 cucumber, diced
- 1/2 red onion, finely chopped
- 1/2 cup fresh parsley, chopped
- 1/4 cup fresh mint, chopped
- 3 tablespoons olive oil
- 2 tablespoons lemon juice
- Salt and pepper, to taste

**Instructions:**

1. In a bowl, soak the bulgur wheat in warm water for 15-20 minutes. Drain any excess water and fluff with a fork.
2. Add the diced tomatoes, cucumber, red onion, parsley, and mint to the bulgur.
3. In a small bowl, whisk together olive oil, lemon juice, salt, and pepper.
4. Pour the dressing over the salad and toss gently. Serve chilled.

## South African Potato Salad

**Ingredients:**

- 6 medium potatoes, boiled and diced
- 1/2 cup mayonnaise
- 2 tablespoons mustard
- 1/4 cup pickles, chopped
- 1/4 cup fresh parsley, chopped
- 1/4 red onion, finely chopped
- Salt and pepper, to taste

**Instructions:**

1. In a large bowl, combine the boiled potatoes, mayonnaise, mustard, pickles, parsley, and red onion.
2. Stir gently to combine, and season with salt and pepper to taste.
3. Chill for at least 30 minutes before serving.

## Swedish Creamy Cabbage Salad

**Ingredients:**

- 4 cups shredded cabbage
- 1/2 cup sour cream
- 2 tablespoons mayonnaise
- 1 tablespoon apple cider vinegar
- 1 teaspoon sugar
- Salt and pepper, to taste

**Instructions:**

1. In a large bowl, combine the shredded cabbage, sour cream, mayonnaise, apple cider vinegar, and sugar.
2. Stir gently to combine and season with salt and pepper to taste.
3. Chill before serving.

## Indonesian Gado-Gado Salad

**Ingredients:**

- 1 cup cooked green beans
- 2 boiled potatoes, diced
- 1/2 cucumber, sliced
- 2 hard-boiled eggs, sliced
- 1/2 cup tofu, fried and cubed
- 1/4 cup peanut sauce (store-bought or homemade)
- 1/4 cup fried shallots (optional)
- Fresh cilantro for garnish

**Instructions:**

1. In a large bowl, combine the green beans, boiled potatoes, cucumber, hard-boiled eggs, and tofu.
2. Drizzle the peanut sauce over the salad and toss gently.
3. Garnish with fried shallots and fresh cilantro before serving.

## Hawaiian Ahi Poke Salad

**Ingredients:**

- 1 lb fresh ahi tuna, cubed
- 1/2 cup soy sauce
- 1 tablespoon sesame oil
- 1 teaspoon rice vinegar
- 1 teaspoon honey
- 1 tablespoon sesame seeds
- 1/2 cucumber, sliced thinly
- 1 avocado, diced
- 1/4 cup green onions, sliced
- 1 tablespoon seaweed (wakame or nori)
- 1/4 teaspoon red pepper flakes (optional)

**Instructions:**

1. In a bowl, mix the soy sauce, sesame oil, rice vinegar, honey, sesame seeds, and red pepper flakes (if using).
2. Add the cubed ahi tuna and toss to coat. Let it marinate for 15-20 minutes.
3. In a serving dish, layer the cucumber, avocado, and green onions.
4. Spoon the marinated tuna over the vegetables and garnish with seaweed.
5. Serve chilled.

**Malaysian Rojak Salad**

**Ingredients:**

- 1 cup pineapple, diced
- 1 cup cucumber, julienned
- 1/2 cup jicama, julienned
- 1/2 cup mango, julienned
- 1/4 cup roasted peanuts, crushed
- 1 tablespoon sugar
- 2 tablespoons tamarind paste
- 2 tablespoons soy sauce
- 1 tablespoon rice vinegar
- 1/2 teaspoon chili paste or fresh chilies (optional)
- Fresh cilantro for garnish

**Instructions:**

1. In a bowl, combine the pineapple, cucumber, jicama, and mango.
2. In a small bowl, whisk together sugar, tamarind paste, soy sauce, rice vinegar, and chili paste.
3. Pour the dressing over the fruits and vegetables and toss to combine.
4. Garnish with crushed peanuts and fresh cilantro before serving.

## Belgian Endive Salad

### Ingredients:

- 4 Belgian endive, sliced
- 1/4 cup walnuts, toasted
- 1/2 apple, thinly sliced
- 2 tablespoons blue cheese, crumbled
- 2 tablespoons olive oil
- 1 tablespoon balsamic vinegar
- 1 teaspoon Dijon mustard
- Salt and pepper, to taste

### Instructions:

1. In a large bowl, combine the endive, toasted walnuts, apple slices, and blue cheese.
2. In a small bowl, whisk together olive oil, balsamic vinegar, Dijon mustard, salt, and pepper.
3. Drizzle the dressing over the salad and toss gently. Serve immediately.

**Finnish Root Vegetable Salad**

**Ingredients:**

- 2 cups boiled potatoes, diced
- 2 cups boiled carrots, diced
- 1 cup boiled rutabaga, diced
- 1/4 cup pickled herring (optional)
- 1/4 cup red onion, finely chopped
- 1/4 cup sour cream
- 2 tablespoons mayonnaise
- 1 tablespoon Dijon mustard
- Salt and pepper, to taste

**Instructions:**

1. In a large bowl, combine the boiled potatoes, carrots, rutabaga, pickled herring, and red onion.
2. In a small bowl, mix together the sour cream, mayonnaise, Dijon mustard, salt, and pepper.
3. Toss the dressing with the root vegetables and chill for at least 30 minutes before serving.

## Australian Beetroot and Goat Cheese Salad

**Ingredients:**

- 2 medium beets, roasted and sliced
- 1/4 cup goat cheese, crumbled
- 1/4 cup arugula or mixed greens
- 1/4 cup walnuts, toasted
- 1 tablespoon olive oil
- 1 tablespoon balsamic vinegar
- Salt and pepper, to taste

**Instructions:**

1. On a serving plate, arrange the roasted beets, goat cheese, and arugula.
2. Drizzle with olive oil and balsamic vinegar, and season with salt and pepper.
3. Top with toasted walnuts and serve immediately.

## Argentine Grilled Corn Salad

**Ingredients:**

- 2 ears of corn, husked and grilled
- 1/2 red onion, diced
- 1/2 red bell pepper, diced
- 1/2 cup fresh cilantro, chopped
- 1/4 cup crumbled feta cheese
- 2 tablespoons olive oil
- 1 tablespoon lime juice
- Salt and pepper, to taste

**Instructions:**

1. Grill the corn until lightly charred, about 10-15 minutes, turning occasionally.
2. Once cooled, cut the kernels off the cob and place them in a bowl.
3. Add the red onion, red bell pepper, cilantro, and feta cheese.
4. Drizzle with olive oil and lime juice, and season with salt and pepper.
5. Toss and serve immediately.

## Chilean Avocado and Tomato Salad

**Ingredients:**

- 2 ripe avocados, diced
- 2 tomatoes, diced
- 1/4 red onion, thinly sliced
- 1 tablespoon olive oil
- 1 tablespoon lemon juice
- 1/4 teaspoon cumin
- Salt and pepper, to taste

**Instructions:**

1. In a bowl, combine the diced avocados, tomatoes, and red onion.
2. Drizzle with olive oil and lemon juice, then sprinkle with cumin, salt, and pepper.
3. Toss gently and serve immediately.

## Dutch Apple Salad

**Ingredients:**

- 2 apples, thinly sliced
- 1/4 cup celery, chopped
- 1/4 cup walnuts, chopped
- 1/4 cup raisins
- 1/2 cup Greek yogurt
- 1 tablespoon honey
- 1 teaspoon lemon juice
- Salt and pepper, to taste

**Instructions:**

1. In a bowl, combine the sliced apples, celery, walnuts, and raisins.
2. In a small bowl, mix together the Greek yogurt, honey, lemon juice, salt, and pepper.
3. Toss the dressing with the apple mixture and serve chilled.

## Middle Eastern Lentil Salad

**Ingredients:**

- 1 cup cooked green or brown lentils
- 1/2 red onion, finely chopped
- 1 cucumber, diced
- 1/2 cup fresh parsley, chopped
- 1/4 cup olive oil
- 2 tablespoons lemon juice
- 1 teaspoon ground cumin
- Salt and pepper, to taste

**Instructions:**

1. In a bowl, combine the cooked lentils, red onion, cucumber, and parsley.
2. In a small bowl, whisk together olive oil, lemon juice, ground cumin, salt, and pepper.
3. Pour the dressing over the lentil mixture and toss well to combine.
4. Serve chilled or at room temperature.

## New Zealand Kumara Salad

**Ingredients:**

- 2 medium kumara (sweet potatoes), peeled and diced
- 1/4 cup olive oil
- 1 tablespoon honey
- 1 teaspoon ground cinnamon
- 1/4 cup feta cheese, crumbled
- 1/4 cup fresh mint, chopped
- 1 tablespoon lemon juice
- Salt and pepper, to taste

**Instructions:**

1. Preheat the oven to 400°F (200°C). Toss the diced kumara with olive oil, honey, cinnamon, salt, and pepper.
2. Roast in the oven for 20-25 minutes, or until tender and slightly caramelized.
3. Let the kumara cool slightly before transferring to a bowl.
4. Add feta cheese, fresh mint, and a drizzle of lemon juice. Toss gently and serve warm or at room temperature.

## Canadian Caesar Salad

**Ingredients:**

- 1 large romaine lettuce, chopped
- 1/4 cup Caesar dressing
- 1/4 cup Parmesan cheese, grated
- 1/4 cup croutons
- Fresh ground black pepper, to taste

**Instructions:**

1. In a large bowl, toss the chopped lettuce with Caesar dressing.
2. Sprinkle with grated Parmesan cheese and top with croutons.
3. Season with freshly ground black pepper to taste.
4. Serve immediately.

## Egyptian Tabbouleh

**Ingredients:**

- 1 cup bulgur wheat
- 2 medium tomatoes, diced
- 1 cucumber, diced
- 1/4 cup fresh parsley, chopped
- 1/4 cup fresh mint, chopped
- 2 tablespoons olive oil
- 2 tablespoons lemon juice
- Salt and pepper, to taste

**Instructions:**

1. Prepare the bulgur wheat according to package instructions. Once cooked, allow it to cool.
2. In a large bowl, combine the cooled bulgur, tomatoes, cucumber, parsley, and mint.
3. Drizzle with olive oil and lemon juice, then season with salt and pepper.
4. Toss gently and serve chilled.

## Colombian Mango Salad

**Ingredients:**

- 2 ripe mangos, peeled and diced
- 1/2 red onion, thinly sliced
- 1/2 avocado, diced
- 1/4 cup fresh cilantro, chopped
- 1 tablespoon lime juice
- Salt and pepper, to taste

**Instructions:**

1. In a bowl, combine the diced mango, red onion, avocado, and cilantro.
2. Drizzle with lime juice and season with salt and pepper.
3. Toss gently and serve immediately.

## Turkish Lentil Salad

**Ingredients:**

- 1 cup cooked red lentils
- 1/2 red onion, finely chopped
- 1/2 cup cucumber, diced
- 1/4 cup fresh parsley, chopped
- 2 tablespoons olive oil
- 2 tablespoons lemon juice
- 1 teaspoon ground cumin
- Salt and pepper, to taste

**Instructions:**

1. In a bowl, combine the cooked lentils, red onion, cucumber, and parsley.
2. In a small bowl, whisk together olive oil, lemon juice, ground cumin, salt, and pepper.
3. Pour the dressing over the lentil mixture and toss well to combine.
4. Serve chilled or at room temperature.

**Indian Chana Salad**

**Ingredients:**

- 1 can chickpeas, drained and rinsed
- 1/2 cucumber, diced
- 1 small tomato, diced
- 1/4 red onion, finely chopped
- 1/4 cup fresh cilantro, chopped
- 1 tablespoon lemon juice
- 1 teaspoon ground cumin
- 1/2 teaspoon ground coriander
- Salt and pepper, to taste

**Instructions:**

1. In a bowl, combine the chickpeas, cucumber, tomato, red onion, and cilantro.
2. In a small bowl, mix the lemon juice, cumin, coriander, salt, and pepper.
3. Pour the dressing over the salad and toss gently.
4. Serve immediately or chill before serving.

## Mexican Cucumber and Lime Salad

**Ingredients:**

- 2 cucumbers, peeled and sliced
- 1 tablespoon olive oil
- 1 tablespoon lime juice
- 1/4 teaspoon chili powder
- Salt, to taste
- Fresh cilantro, chopped (optional)

**Instructions:**

1. In a large bowl, combine the sliced cucumbers with olive oil and lime juice.
2. Sprinkle with chili powder and salt.
3. Toss gently and garnish with fresh cilantro, if desired.
4. Serve immediately.

www.ingramcontent.com/pod-product-compliance
Lightning Source LLC
LaVergne TN
LVHW061957070526
838199LV00060B/4169